ART OF CREATING ORIGAMI ART

'ART OF CREATING VARIOUS TYPES OF ORIGAMI ART'

DR. NIMISH TOMAR

CONTENTS

CHAPTER 1

The Origami art is the an traditional Japanese art of creating objects from single piece of paper by using the technique of folding paper into a variety of decorative forms.

The various decorative forms of art that are created by using paper includes the following:

Animals

Flowers

The art of Origami helps the students and the kids in improving their skills sets.

In the modern-day classroom the art of Origami helps the students in the following aspects:

Teaching geometry

Thinking skills,

Fractions

Problem solving

Fun science

Education

Development and Therapy

Eye hand co-ordination

Sequencing skills

Maths reasoning

Spatial skills

Memory

Patience

Attention skills

Fine motor skills

Mental concentration

Learning about other cultures

Working together

Teaching

Measurement

Proportions

Symmetry

Geometry

3D Comprehension

Sequencing

Problem Solving

**Cooperative learning where
children learn to work together
and support each other.**

**Learn about other cultures
and communities.**

Patience

Sence of achievement

Community building

Sense of achievement

Besides the benefits as mentioned above the art of Origami is also used in therapeutic settings. The art of Origami the following therapeutical benefits:

Mental stimulus with exercise

Physical stimulus with exercise

Art therapy

Stroke rehabilitation

Injury rehabilitation

◆ ◆ ◆

CHAPTER 2

TYPES OF ORIGAMI ART

The types of origami art are as follows:

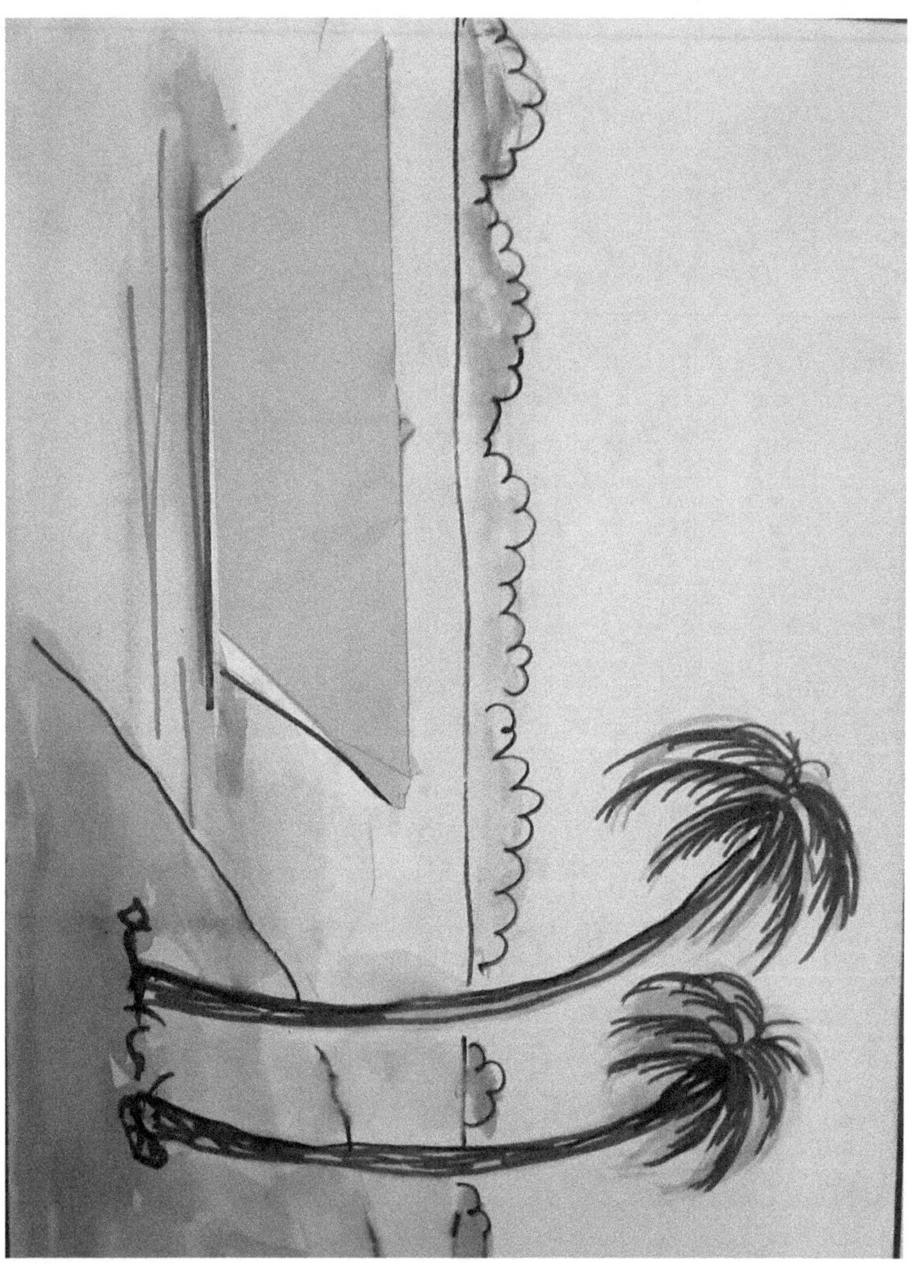

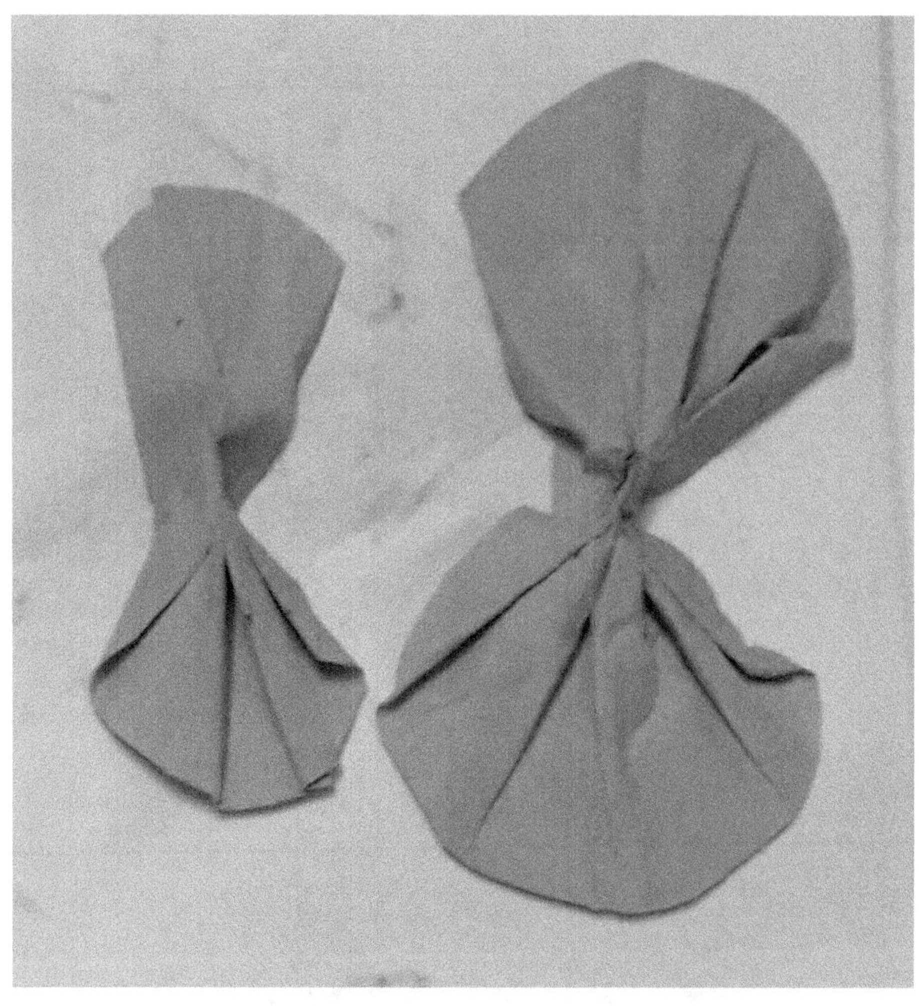

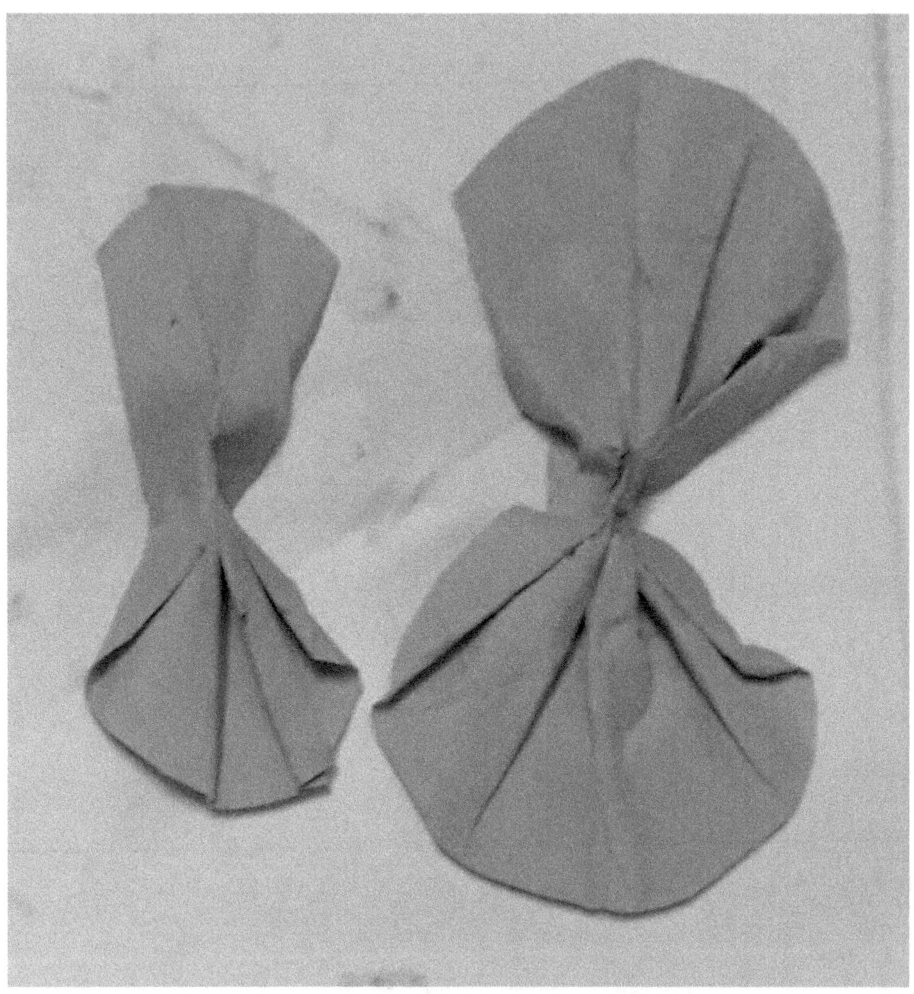

The